D1377305

POISONINGS

JON SUTHERLAND
AND
DIANE CANWELL

A⁺

Smart Apple Media

This book has been published in cooperation with Arcturus Publishing Limited.

The right of Jon Sutherland and Diane Canwell to be identified as the authors of this work has been asserted by them in accordance with the Copyright, Designs and Patents Act 1988.

Series concept: Alex Woolf
Editor and picture researcher: Alex Woolf
Designer: Tall Tree

The artwork on page 36 is by Jason Line.

Library of Congress Cataloging-in-Publication Data

Sutherland, Jonathan.
  Poisonings / John Sutherland and Diane Canwell.
    p. cm. – (Solve it with science)
  Includes index.
  ISBN 978-1-59920-332-4 (hardcover)
  1. Poisoning–Juvenile literature. 2. Poisoners–Juvenile literature. 3. Murder–Juvenile literature. I. Canwell, Diane. II. Title.
  HV6553.S88 2010
  364.152'3–dc22
                                      2009002339

9 8 7 6 5 4 3 2 1

Picture credits:
Arcturus: 36.
Canwell, Diane and Jon Sutherland: 8.
Corbis: 6 (Sankei Shimbun/Corbis Sygma), 16 (Jean Pimental/Kipa), 17 (Interpress/Sygma), 24 (Handout/Reuters), 42 (Sebastian Widmann/epa).
FLPA: 10 (Parameswaran Pillai Karunakaran).
Getty Images: 11 (Fox Photos/Stringer), cover *right* and 12 (Keystone/Stringer), 14 (Keystone/Stringer), 20 (Handout), 32 (Erik S Lesser/Stringer).
Rex Features: 18 (Sipa Press), 27 (Brian Harris), 40 (Francesco Guidicini), 43 (Kommersant/Keystone).
Science Photo Library: 4 (Sheila Terry), 5 (Colin Cuthbert), 7 (Mauro Fermariello), 29 (Mauro Fermariello), 30 (Dr Jurgen Scriba), 33 (Charles D Winters), 34–35 (Dr Jurgen Scriba), 38–39 (Klaus Guldbrandsen), 41 (Rich Treptow).
Shutterstock: cover *left* (Gareth Howlett), 9 (ANP), 13 (Darla Hallmark), 15 (Paul Reid), 19 (Ivaschenko Roman), 21 (Eric Isselée), 25 (stocksnapp), 26 (ultimathule), 37 (Kheng Guan Toh).
TopFoto: 22 (Universal Picture Press), 23 (Universal Picture Press).
Wikimedia Commons: 28 (Dschwen).

Every attempt has been made to clear copyright. Should there be any inadvertent omission, please apply to the publisher for rectification.

All words in **bold** may be found in the glossary on pages 46–47.

CONTENTS

INTRODUCTION

Poisoning was a common method of murder during the nineteenth century. In several famous murder cases, **arsenic or strychnine** was added to food. Poisoning was difficult to detect in Victorian times. The police lacked the knowledge and equipment. For example, they could tell that arsenic or **cyanide** had been used, but they could not say how much had been used. Neither could they tell how long the victim had been receiving the poison.

Antique bottles of poison

WHAT IS A FORENSIC TOXICOLOGIST?

A **forensic** toxicologist is an expert in poisons and their effects on the body. Today, **toxicologists** play an important part in murder investigations. They can test samples of blood, body fluids, tissues, and organs for the presence of poisons. They can help identify the type of poison used and determine how it got into the body.

Forensic toxicologists are not only needed by the police. They can assist the doctors in cases of accidental poisoning. They can help identify the poison used and suggest treatment for it.

4

DRUG TESTS

Toxicologists can also test for different kinds of drugs that can affect the human body. These may be prescribed by a doctor or taken illegally. In a drug-related crime, the toxicologist will take samples of blood and/or urine from the victim and the suspect to test for drugs. This will help determine if there were drugs in the victim's body and whether the suspect was under the influence of drugs when the crime was committed. Alcohol is considered to be a drug because it can affect the way someone behaves.

TESTING FOR ARSENIC

Arsenic is a poison that is present in the soil. If the body of a suspected poison victim is exhumed, soil samples should be taken from all sides of the grave. The toxicologist's tests might show that there is more arsenic in the body than there is in the surrounding soil. This would help to prove that the arsenic could not have entered the body through the soil.

A toxicologist studies the effects of chemicals on a sample of human muscle tissue.

As well as analyzing the stomach contents for poison or drugs, toxicologists also test the organs of the body. Poisons and drugs can affect every organ in the body. They can test tissue samples from the liver, kidneys, stomach, heart, and lungs.

SAMPLES FOR STUDY

When a murder scene is discovered, the scene is examined carefully for clues. The body is taken away for an **autopsy** to be carried out by a **pathologist**. The pathologist's job is to determine how and when the murder took place. The pathologist is assisted by a forensic toxicologist. Specimens of body tissues and fluids are sent to the toxicologist for examination.

Often, the forensic toxicologist is given just a tiny sample from the murder scene to work on.

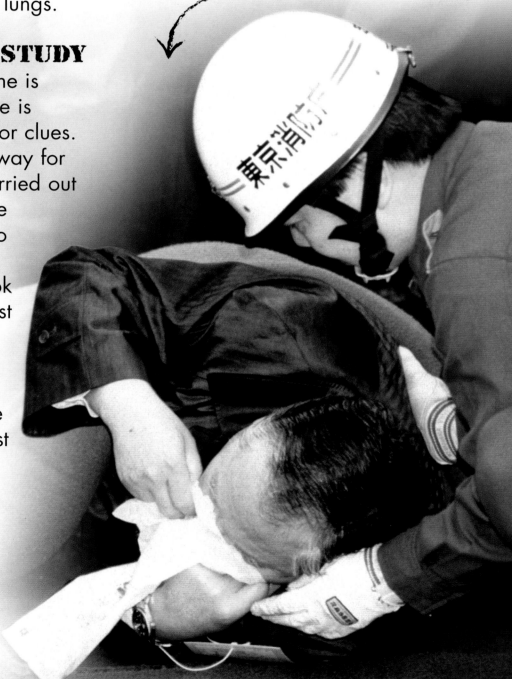

A victim of poisoning is assisted by a member of the emergency services in Tokyo, Japan. In 1995, a secret religious organization released poisonous sarin gas in the Tokyo subway system.

This might be a drop of blood, a fingernail, or a hair. From this, it will be determined whether or not drugs or poisons are present, what they are, and if they were the cause of death.

FORENSIC TESTS

Forensic toxicologists use a range of different tests to detect and identify the presence of drugs or poisons. One test, called **chromatography**, involves separating the components of mixtures in order to identify them. Another test, spectrography, identifies substances such as poisons by passing light through them. Toxicologists also use an instrument called a scanning electron microscope to scan the surface of metal fragments, paint, ink, hair, and fibers. The toxicologist can match samples found on a suspect's clothing with those found at the crime scene.

Pathologists dissect a corpse during an autopsy to discover the cause of death.

EXPERT WITNESSES

Toxicologists often appear in court as expert witnesses. They may be asked to describe, for example, what drug was found and in what quantity, when the drug entered the body, and how.

THE CLUE WAS IN THE DOG

Arthur and Ethel Lillie Major married in 1918. They set up home in the village of Kirkby-on-Bain, UK. In May 1934, Ethel discovered that Arthur was seeing another woman. The woman, Rose Kettleborough, lived nearby.

Arthur became worried about his wife. He told some of his friends at the gravel pit where he worked that he thought Ethel was trying to poison him.

Ethel Lillie Major

SANDWICHES

On May 22, Ethel made Arthur some corned beef sandwiches. While he was eating them, he told his friends that he thought they tasted bad. He felt so ill that he left work. When he arrived home, he threw the sandwiches on the floor. The neighbor's dog ate the sandwiches.

The following day, the dog died and was buried. Arthur, who was feeling much worse, began having convulsions. The local doctor thought that Arthur was having an epileptic seizure and gave him a sedative. Ethel told the doctor that Arthur had been having these spasms for a year or two.

CAUSE OF DEATH?

Arthur died during the night. The doctor was surprised to hear of the death. He gave the official cause of death as epilepsy. In fact, Arthur had shown the classic symptoms of strychnine poisoning.

The neighbor's dog was an accidental victim of Ethel Major's plot to kill her husband.

EFFECTS OF STRYCHNINE

If strychnine gets into the body, the effects can begin within an hour. Victims show signs of being agitated and easily frightened. They experience muscle spasms, and their arms and legs become rigid. Victims also have difficulty breathing.

MYSTERY LETTER

Two days later, while Ethel was organizing Arthur's funeral, the local police received an anonymous letter. It read:

Sir, have you heard of a wife poisoning her husband? Look no further into the death of Mr. Major of Kirkby-on-Bain. Why did he complain of his food tasting nasty and throw it to a neighbor's dog, which has since died? Ask the undertaker if he looked natural after death. Why did he stiffen so quickly? Why was he so jerky when dying? I myself have heard her threaten to poison him years ago. In the name of the law, I beg you to analyze the contents of his stomach.

DIGGING UP THE BODIES

The police moved quickly. Chief Inspector Hugh Young led the investigation. He stopped Arthur's funeral from taking place. The police called in a pathologist from London to examine Arthur's body. They also had the body of the neighbor's dog **exhumed**.

Arthur and the dog showed signs of strychnine poisoning.

The leaves and berries of the Strychnos nux-vomica tree are the most common source of the poison strychnine.

ANALYZING STOMACH CONTENTS

It can take between 24 and 48 hours for the stomach to completely break down food. Even after someone has died, it is possible to tell what his or her last meal was. A toxicologist can also determine if the person had taken or been given any drugs. This is why it is important to analyze stomach contents when poisoning is suspected.

LOOKING FOR PROOF

Chief Inspector Young began to question Ethel, who claimed that she had no access to strychnine. The police could find no sign of strychnine in the Majors' house. The chief inspector was certain that Ethel had put the strychnine in Arthur's corned beef sandwiches. But he needed proof to prove it in court.

Eventually, the police found out that Ethel's father had used strychnine to kill rats and mice. They questioned him and he told them that Ethel had a key to the locked box where he kept the strychnine.

Ethel Lillie Major was brought to trial and found guilty on November 1, 1934. She was hanged on December 19, in Hull Prison.

Norman Birkett (later Lord Birkett) was the lawyer who defended Ethel Lillie Major at her trial at Lincoln Assizes.

A PASSION FOR POISON

Graham Young was born in London on September 7, 1947. His mother died three months after he was born. Young then lived with his aunt. He didn't have many friends, and preferred to read books about black magic, forensics, and toxicology. When he was 14, he took his interest in toxicology too far.

Graham Young

FIRST VICTIMS

Young's first victim was a friend from school, Christopher Williams. Williams didn't die but became very ill in 1961. Around the same time, some of Young's family became ill. His sister Winifred began to suffer from stomach cramps and vomiting. Tests done that November showed she had been poisoned with **belladonna**, a toxic plant.

Later, Young's stepmother became seriously ill. She died on April 21, 1962. Years later, scientists discovered that she also had been poisoned with belladonna but had grown immune to it. On the night before her death, Young had given his stepmother another kind of poison—**thallium**.

Young's next victim was his father, Fred. Fred was admitted to a hospital after complaining of illness. He was diagnosed with **antimony** poisoning. Around the same time, Young's chemistry teacher grew suspicious and searched his desk. In it, the teacher found poisons and books on poisons. He contacted the police.

ARRESTED

Young was arrested and sent to a police **psychiatrist**. Young admitted he had poisoned his friends and family out of curiosity to see how their bodies would react to the poisons. Young was sent to Broadmoor maximum security hospital.

In June of 1970, the prison psychiatrist concluded that Young was cured of his obsession with poisoning people. Young was released on February 4, 1971.

WHAT IS BELLADONNA?

Belladonna is one of the world's most toxic plants. All parts of the plant are poisonous. It causes irregular heartbeat and breathing. Even dogs and cats can be affected by belladonna if they eat it.

The belladonna is also known as deadly nightshade.

John Tilson was a workmate of Graham Young and one of his victims. Fortunately, Tilson survived.

He died shortly after being admitted. Fred Briggs, another employee, died in November.

A total of 70 people employed at the factory had been ill with similar symptoms. When the factory's doctor tried to reassure them that everything was fine, Young interrupted him. He asked why thallium poisoning had not been considered a cause of the deaths. It seemed Young was still wanting to boast about his poisoning abilities, no matter the cost. The doctor grew suspicious of Young and called the police.

SICKNESS AT WORK

Young found work at a photographic processing factory in May 1971. The factory used the chemical thallium. Young started serving his coworkers tea. Soon, several of his coworkers and his boss started feeling ill when they were at work. They suffered from severe stomach cramps and dizziness. Young's boss, Bob Egle, was admitted to a hospital in July.

EFFECTS OF THALLIUM ON THE BODY

Thallium poisoning can cause stomach cramps, vomiting, and diarrhea. Victims usually lose hair and their skin thickens and becomes scaly.

CAUGHT IN POSSESSION

Young was arrested when police found thallium in his pocket. At his apartment, police found enough thallium and antimony to kill hundreds of people. He was charged with two murders, two attempted murders, and two acts of poisoning. He pleaded not guilty to all charges.

Forensic science had the advantage over Young. The bodies of his victims were exhumed. In the autopsies, pathologists found symptoms of poisoning, but no traces of the poison. Ten days later, they located the traces of poison in the organs.

The ashes of Bob Egle were investigated and traces of thallium were found. This was the first case where ashes were exhumed and analyzed.

GUILTY

Young was found guilty and given four life sentences. Young died in Parkhurst Prison on August 1, 1990.

Graham Young had been making tea laced with thallium and antimony for his coworkers. He became known as the Teacup Poisoner.

THE BLACK WIDOW OF LOUDUN

Marie Besnard, a 52-year-old widow of Loudun, France, was arrested in July 1949. Between 1927 and 1947, a total of 13 of Besnard's family and friends had died. She was charged with poisoning her mother, father, both her husbands, her father-in-law, mother-in-law, sister-in-law, grandmother-in-law, two cousins, a great aunt, and two friends.

SUSPICIOUS DEATHS

They had died, apparently, of unrelated causes, including pneumonia, suicide, and eating poisoned mushrooms. Each person had left Besnard some money. One of the last to die was her second husband, Léon. Before he died, he had told a friend he thought he was being poisoned.

Suspicions were aroused and the police were called in. All 13 bodies were exhumed and examined by toxicologist Georges Beroud. He discovered that all the bodies contained high levels of arsenic.

A recreation of the death of Léon Besnard, with his wife and doctor looking on, from the French film L'Affaire Marie Besnard *(1986).*

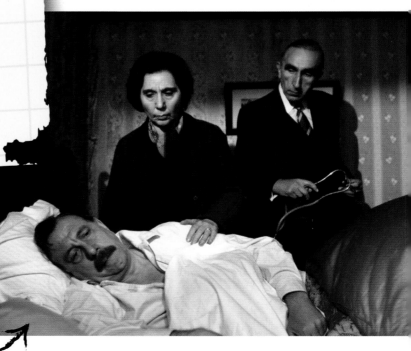

Marie Besnard appears in court during her second trial in March 1954.

RETRIAL

At Besnard's trial in 1952, her defense lawyer argued that Beroud had been careless in his techniques. The trial ended without a verdict. At a second trial, expert witnesses claimed that arsenic was present in the soil and could have entered the dead bodies, through the hair, from the surrounding earth. Another investigation was ordered to prove that the arsenic was in the bodies before they were buried. This investigation involved the examination of the hair using a technique called neutron activation analysis.

NEUTRON ACTIVATION ANALYSIS

The scientists analyzed the concentration of arsenic in the samples of hair by bombarding them with neutrons (particles from the nucleus of an atom). This made the **isotopes** in the arsenic unstable. These isotopes were then measured for their gamma ray emissions (a kind of **nuclear radiation**). The gamma ray emissions had to be analyzed for at least 26.5 hours to measure the concentration of arsenic.

NOT GUILTY

In the end, forensic techniques were unable to prove that Marie Besnard had actually given her relatives the arsenic. After three separate trials, she was found not guilty on December 12, 1961. She died in 1980, aged 83.

THE SHE-DEVIL OF NANCY

In July 1977, Marcel Fixard, a retired French army officer, began a relationship with Simone Weber, a 54-year-old widow from Nancy, France. Three years later, Weber used a stolen prescription to obtain the poisonous drug digitalis. Soon after this, Fixard became very ill. Despite advice to take him to the hospital, Weber did nothing. On May 14, 1980, the 80-year-old Fixard died of a heart attack.

Simone Weber in 1991

JEALOUS

In 1981, Weber began a relationship with Bernard Hettier. But Hettier had other girlfriends, and Weber became jealous. Hettier told his friends he was sure that Weber was slowly poisoning him. On June 22, 1985, Hettier disappeared.

The police made enquiries and found that Weber's husband had died in suspicious circumstances. In February 1986, a judge ordered the exhumation of Fixard. No digitalis was found in his body. Digitalis disappears some years after death.

Flowers of the foxglove plant, Digitalis purpurea, *the source of the drug digitalis.*

ANOTHER BODY

Soon after the exhumation, a suitcase was discovered floating in the River Marne. It contained the remains of Bernard Hettier. Suspicion immediately focused on Weber. She was accused of drugging and shooting him, then cutting him up and putting him in the suitcase. The police searched Weber's homes and found guns, cartridges, and a circular saw. The saw contained traces of human tissue.

Throughout the trial, Weber pleaded not guilty to murder. She claimed that she had bought the digitalis for herself because she suffered from a heart problem. However, five doctors asserted that she had no such heart problem.

The jury took 11 hours to reach a decision. Eventually, they found Weber not guilty of poisoning Fixard, but guilty of murdering Hettier. She was sentenced to 20 years in prison.

EFFECT OF DIGITALIS ON THE BODY

Digitalis comes from the foxglove plant. Just a small nibble of the plant can make someone ill. If taken in large amounts, digitalis can seriously affect the heart rate and cause death. Unlike arsenic, digitalis disappears completely some years after death.

THE KILLER DOCTOR

In the 1970s, Harold Shipman was a doctor working at a practice in West Yorkshire, England. When he started to suffer from blackouts, he told his partners he was suffering from epilepsy. In truth, he had been forging the prescriptions to obtain the epileptic drug pethidine. The drug had caused his blackouts. When his addiction was discovered, Shipman was sent to a drug rehabilitation center and he lost his job.

Harold Shipman

24, 1998, at the age of 81, her daughter Angela became suspicious. Shipman had been the last person to see Kathleen alive. He told Angela that an autopsy would not be necessary because he had seen Kathleen just before she died.

Angela went to the police and Detective Superintendent Bernard Postles began to investigate. He ordered an exhumation and an autopsy. Grundy's tissue and hair samples were sent to different laboratories for analysis.

SUSPICIOUS DEATH

Two years later, in 1977, Shipman joined a doctors' practice in Hyde, Greater Manchester. Many of his patients began to die unexpectedly. When Kathleen Grundy died on June

FATAL DOSE

Toxicologist Julie Evans gave her report on the cause of Grundy's death. Grundy had received a fatal dose of **morphine** about 3 hours before she died. There was also **insulin** in her body. Grundy was not diabetic and would not have needed insulin.

The police began investigating the deaths of Shipman's other patients. Many of them had died unexpectedly. All of them had seen Shipman on the day they died. The police examined the bodies of 15 of Shipman's former patients.

Morphine is extracted from the poppy plant.

MORPHINE

Morphine is a highly addictive drug, much like heroin. It is one of the few drugs that stays in the body for years after death. It can easily be found during an autopsy.

TESTING FOR DRUGS AND POISONS

Toxicologists examine samples of blood, urine, or tissue. They conduct tests to find out whether a person has died from drugs or poisoning. They add different solutions to the samples. The samples will change color if drugs are present.

Harold Shipman's former office in Hyde, Greater Manchester

Dr. John Rutherford was a government pathologist who gave evidence at Shipman's trial. He told the court about the autopsy results. He said that all the victims had died from morphine toxicity, not old age or natural causes. Rutherford had also taken a set of Grundy's fingerprints when he examined her body. This would help the police to prove Shipman had forged Grundy's will.

FORGED DOCUMENTS

The police suspected that Shipman was motivated by greed. Grundy had left Shipman approximately $630,000. Had Shipman forged her will? Forensic scientists examined the will. They found three sets of fingerprints on it: Shipman's and those of the two witnesses who signed it. Grundy's fingerprints were not on her will, so she had never touched it.

The police found a typewriter in Shipman's house that he had used to forge the will. Shipman had also forged many patients' records. The records had been stored on his computer. He changed them after he had murdered a patient so that it appeared they had been suffering from an illness.

GUILTY

Harold Shipman was found guilty of murdering 15 of his patients. He was also found guilty of forgery. The judge gave him 15 life sentences and a four-year sentence for forgery. The judge recommended that Shipman remain in prison for the rest of his life.

On January 13, 2004, Harold Shipman committed suicide in Wakefield Prison by hanging himself in his cell.

Hyde Cemetery in Greater Manchester. Human remains were exhumed from this cemetery to provide evidence in the case of Harold Shipman.

THE UMBRELLA MURDER

Georgi Markov was a Bulgarian writer and broadcaster. He left Bulgaria in 1969 and began work in London for the BBC World Service in 1971. This was the time of the **Cold War** between the **Soviet Union**, the United States, and their respective allies. Bulgaria was an ally of the Soviet Union and an enemy of the West. Markov was a fierce critic of the Bulgarian government.

Georgi Markov often criticized the Bulgarian government in his writings. He died in 1978 after a stranger stabbed him with a poison-tipped umbrella.

A SHARP PAIN

On September 7, 1978, Markov was traveling from his home in Clapham, southwest London, to his office at Bush House. He walked from Waterloo Station to a bus stop on the south side of the Waterloo Bridge. While he waited for his bus, he felt a sharp jab in the back of his right thigh, followed by a stinging pain.

It was lunchtime and the pavement was crowded, but Markov saw a man picking up an umbrella close to him. The man apologized in a foreign accent, then quickly jumped into a taxi. Markov continued to his office.

FEELING ILL

Markov began to work but started to feel ill as the day went on. He did not know it then, but he was suffering from **ricin** poisoning.

Ricin is obtained from the seeds of the castor oil plant (Ricinus communis). The seeds are enclosed within the plant's spiny fruits.

THE EFFECTS OF RICIN

Ricin is highly toxic. It comes from the seeds of the castor oil plant. Ricin contains two toxins. The first toxin enters the body's cells and allows the second toxin to travel within it. The second toxin attacks the cells and kills them off. Once the ricin reaches the bloodstream, it quickly spreads through the body. Ricin causes the organs to stop functioning. It also makes the body's **white cell count** rise dramatically. There is no other poison that produces such a high white cell count.

When Markov arrived home that night, he told his wife Annabel about his leg. When they looked at his thigh, they saw it had a small mark on it, similar to a mark left by a **hypodermic needle**.

BLOOD POISONING

That night, Markov developed a fever. The next day he was admitted to a hospital. The doctors found a small wound in his thigh and diagnosed blood poisoning. Markov died in the hospital three days later. He was 49 years old.

Markov had told the police that he thought he had been poisoned. When he died, they ordered an autopsy. Forensic scientists looked at samples of Markov's blood. They concluded that Markov had been killed by a tiny pellet containing the poison ricin. The poison could only be identified because it had not dissolved completely.

WAX-COVERED PELLET

The scientists believed that the pellet may have been coated with a wax. The wax melted when it entered Markov's body. The pellet had two tiny holes drilled into it, and the ricin was inside the holes. Some think that the ricin pellet was fired in a dart from the umbrella tip into Markov's leg.

An umbrella similar to this one was used to kill Georgi Markov.

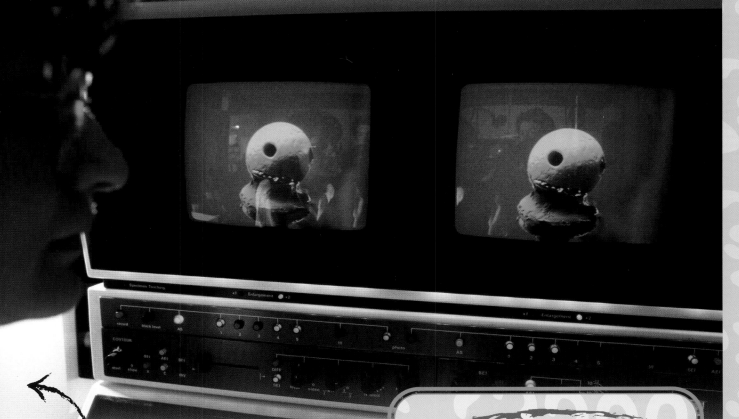

A researcher at the Police Forensic Science Services Laboratory in London examines the pellet used in Markov's murder.

Others think a hypodermic needle was used to inject the pellet into him when the assassin bent down to pick up an umbrella he had been carrying.

No one has ever been charged with the murder of Georgi Markov. However, it is likely that the murderer was an agent of the Bulgarian or Soviet government.

WHAT DID THE SCIENTISTS DO?

To prove that Georgi Markov had been poisoned with ricin, the scientists injected a pig with the poison. For 6 hours, the animal showed no symptoms of poisoning. Then it developed a high fever. The pig's white cell count began to rise. Within 24 hours, the pig had died. When the scientists did an autopsy on the pig, they found the same organ damage that Georgi Markov had suffered.

27

HEAVY METAL

Robert and Joann Curley lived in Wilkes-Barre, Pennsylvania. Robert went to the hospital in August 1991 with a mysterious illness. He had pain in his legs and felt weak. Robert's skin felt as if it was burning and he was suffering frequent bouts of vomiting. He had also lost a lot of his hair.

By September, Robert's condition was getting worse, and he was put on a life support machine. On September 27, 1991, Joann Curley agreed with the doctors that the life support machine should be turned off, and Robert died.

THALLIUM

The doctors had carried out tests on Curley while he was in the hospital. Tests showed that Curley's body had high levels of thallium. Because Curley had been an electrician, the police thought he may have come into contact with thallium at work. Yet none of his coworkers experienced symptoms of poisoning. Investigators wondered if a practical joker may have added some thallium salts to Curley's tea as a prank. But this was ruled out when his coworkers were questioned.

A rod of thallium

An autopsy

MURDER

Joann Curley and her daughter also showed some signs of thallium poisoning. But the levels in their bodies were nowhere near as high as those in Robert's body. His autopsy showed such high levels of thallium in his system that the possibility of accidental poisoning was ruled out. His death was reported as murder.

UNDETECTABLE POISON

Thallium is a heavy metal. The salts of the metal are colorless. They are also soluble in water and tasteless. This means that they can be used without the victim noticing. Thallium can be inhaled from dust or fumes. It can also be taken by mouth or absorbed through the skin.

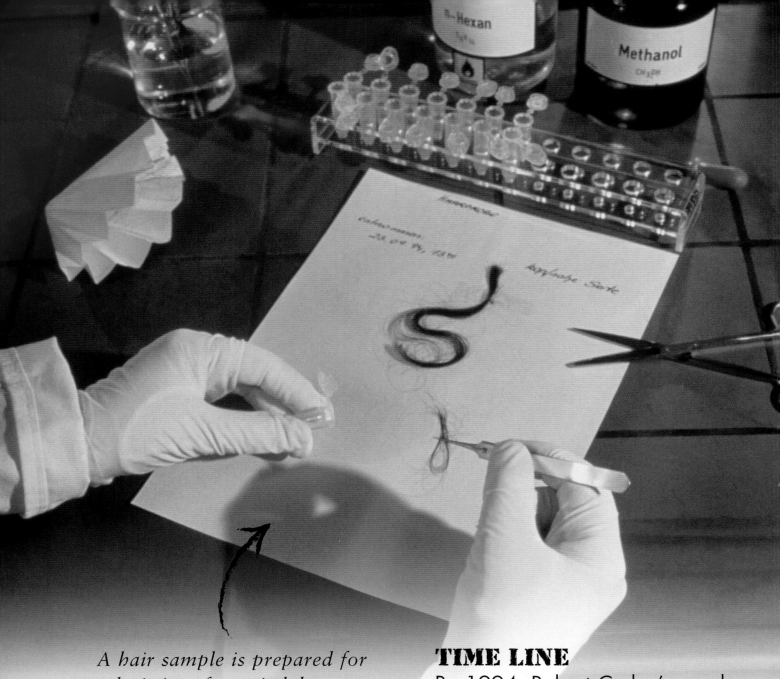

A hair sample is prepared for analysis in a forensic laboratory. As hair grows, it incorporates traces of chemicals produced when drugs and poisons are consumed. These chemicals remain in a fixed position on the hair shaft, revealing a time line of when the poison was taken.

TIME LINE

By 1994, Robert Curley's murder had still not been solved. The police contacted Dr. Frederic Rieders. He ran a private toxicology laboratory in Willow Grove, Pennsylvania. His laboratory was equipped to do a more thorough analysis of samples from Curley's body.

Rieders believed he could produce a time line that would show exactly when the thallium had entered Curley's body.

Curley's body was exhumed. Dr. Rieders took hair, toenail,

WHAT THE TOXICOLOGIST FOUND OUT

Dr. Rieders analyzed hair samples taken from Curley's body. The hair strands were long enough to plot almost the entire final year of Curley's life. The thallium levels were measured over nine months. The toxicologist, with the help of the pathologist, managed to identify each time Curley had been given the thallium. They demonstrated that the thallium had been introduced over a period of time. More importantly, they had identified the actual cause of death.

fingernail, skin, and tissue samples. The samples showed that the thallium levels in Curley's body rose in late 1990. During 1991, the levels went up and down. Then, just before Curley's death in September, they shot up.

ALONE WITH ROBERT

The analysis by Dr. Rieders proved very high levels of thallium entered Curley's body during his stay in the hospital. The investigating team realized that Curley's wife Joann had been alone with him each time the thallium levels had increased. In the final days, when the thallium levels had shot up, Joann had brought him food and been alone with him at his bedside. When Curley died, his wife received $296,000 from an insurance policy.

Joann Curley was arrested and charged with murder. She admitted murdering her husband with thallium in the form of rat poison. She was sentenced to prison for 10–20 years.

ANTIFREEZE

Maurice Glenn Turner was a police officer in Cobb County, Georgia. He married Lynn Womack in 1993. Just six months into their marriage, Lynn became unfaithful and started seeing someone else. His name was Randy Thompson and he was a firefighter. Lynn told him she was divorced.

Lynn Turner at a press conference in 2001

HEART FAILURE

On March 2, 1995, Maurice Turner was admitted to the hospital. He believed he had the flu. He was treated and felt better, so he was sent home. The following day, he died. The doctor who examined his body said that Turner had died of heart failure because of an enlarged heart. He was buried on March 6. Lynn Turner received $153,000 from her late husband's life insurance.

A few days after Maurice Turner's death, Lynn Turner and Randy Thompson moved in together. Over the next three years they had two children, a boy and a girl. Thompson had taken out some life insurance. If anything happened to him, Lynn would receive the insurance money.

The relationship started to go wrong. Thompson moved out of their apartment, but he continued visiting Turner and the children.

In January 2001, Thompson ate a meal at Turner's house. That night, Thompson went to the hospital with flu-like symptoms. He was treated and sent home. Thompson died the following day. The cause of death was stated as heart failure due to clogged arteries.

ODD COINCIDENCE

Thompson's mother was suspicious about her son's death. She contacted Maurice Turner's mother, and they compared the deaths of the two men. They were convinced it was not a coincidence and contacted Dr. Mark Koponen. He was the deputy chief medical examiner of the Georgia Bureau of Investigation.

An autopsy on Thompson's body was carried out by a medical examiner. Traces of **ethylene glycol** were found in his tissues. Ethylene glycol is found in antifreeze.

EFFECTS OF ETHYLENE GLYCOL

Antifreeze is 95 percent ethylene glycol. It is not usually found in the body. If it gets into the body, it can cause headaches, slurred speech, and dizziness. Consuming ethylene glycol ultimately leads to kidney or heart failure.

Antifreeze

33

INDEPENDENT TESTS

The similarity of the two men's deaths aroused the suspicions of the investigators. They exhumed the body of Maurice Turner six years after he had died. An independent laboratory carried out tests on both bodies in 2001.

Forensic scientists working at the lab found ethylene glycol in Turner's body. They also found calcium crystals in the kidney tissues of both men. The only way calcium crystals could be present in a body was if the victim had been given ethylene glycol.

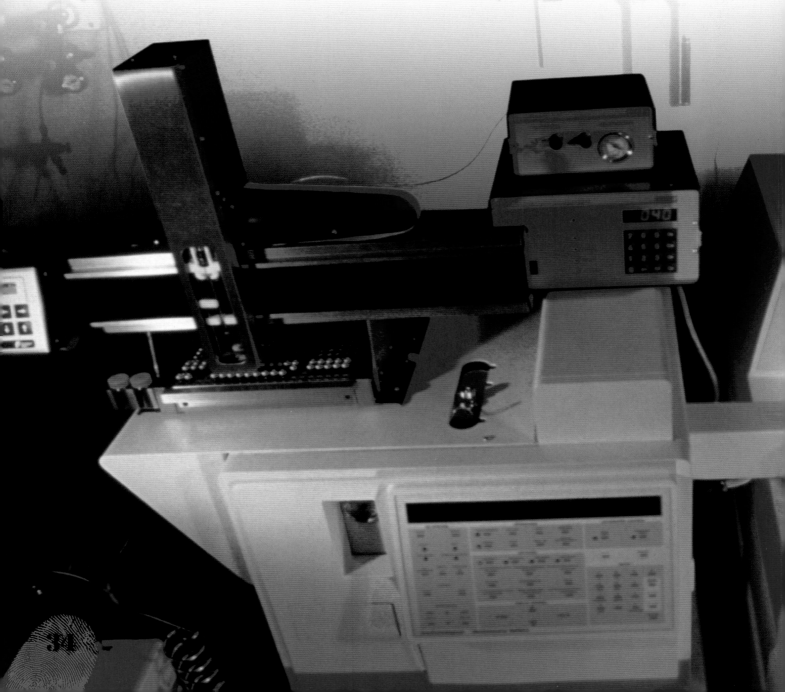

WHAT THE SCIENTISTS DID

The forensic toxicologists tested the blood and urine samples of both bodies. They used a **gas chromatography mass spectrometer**. This instrument separates the different parts of the sample. It identifies any chemicals present in the blood and urine samples. They can tell what the chemicals are by how quickly they evaporate into gases.

TELEVISED TRIAL

Lynn Turner's trial was shown on television. The **prosecution** confirmed that Maurice Turner and Randy Thompson were the only men in Georgia to have died from ethylene glycol poisoning. The medical examiner explained that ethylene glycol has no taste. Therefore, it could have been added to the men's food, in the form of antifreeze, without them noticing.

Lynn Turner insisted on her innocence throughout the trial. Nevertheless, on May 14, 2004, the jury found her guilty of the murder of Maurice Turner. On March 27, 2007, she was also found guilty of murdering Randy Thompson. She was given a sentence of life imprisonment.

A gas chromatography mass spectrometer is sensitive enough to detect minute quantities of abnormal chemicals present in a sample of body fluid.

SOMETHING IN THE CURRY

Masumi Hayashi and her husband Kenji lived in Wakayama, Japan. Masumi sold insurance and Kenji ran an ant extermination business. Kenji used arsenic in his work.

On July 25, 1998, the local community held a summer festival. Masumi offered to help prepare the curry and rice. Hundreds of people were expected and they would all be offered the curry to eat.

Masumi Hayashi

LATE ARRIVAL

A garage close to the Hayashi's home was used as a kitchen to cook the curry. Masumi did not get along with her neighbors. She felt they shunned her and her family. Masumi was late and cooking was already under way when she arrived. She became convinced her neighbors were ignoring her because she was late.

Soon after the curry had been served, people who had eaten it became ill. A total of 67 people were taken to a hospital. They suffered from vomiting, irregular heartbeat, and numbness in their limbs. The following day, four people died. Two of the dead were important people in Wakayama. The other two were children.

ARSENIC

At first, the police thought that the curry had been laced with cyanide. But when more tests were carried out, they discovered traces of arsenic. They were unsure if it was the food or the knives and forks used to eat it that had been poisoned.

Just four people, including Masumi Hayashi, had been left alone while the curry was being prepared. Of the four, only Masumi had access to arsenic through her husband's ant extermination business.

EFFECTS OF ARSENIC

Arsenic is used in pesticides, herbicides, and insecticides. If it enters the body, it can cause death. It stops the body's **enzymes** from working properly, causing the body's organs to stop functioning.

A pot of curry

HOW THE SCIENTISTS FOUND OUT

The police had to prove that the arsenic in the curry was the same as the arsenic used by the ant extermination business. They used a special machine developed in Japan called a synchrotron. They tested powder from the business's stores and powder from the curry. The synchrotron compared the samples and showed that they were identical. Unlike other similar machines, the synchroton does not damage the samples during testing.

ARRESTED

Approximately 200 police officers surrounded the home of Masumi and Kenji to arrest them. They were taken away for questioning, and their home was searched. Masumi was charged with murder and attempted murder. Both Masumi and her husband were also charged with insurance fraud.

During the trial, the prosecution presented evidence to show that Masumi had poisoned, or attempted to poison, other people in the past. She had taken out insurance policies on people she knew. After visiting her house, they had died. Masumi pleaded guilty to the charges of insurance fraud. However, she pleaded not guilty to the charges of murder and attempted murder.

SENTENCED

On December 11, 2002, Masumi Hayashi was found guilty of murdering the four people at the festival. She was also found guilty of injuring 63 others and was sentenced to hang. Kenji was also jailed, but only for insurance fraud.

Arsenic powder is extremely poisonous in large doses and also can be fatal when taken repeatedly in small doses. It is used as a weed killer and as an insecticide.

SOMETHING IN THE TEA

Alexander Litvinenko was born in the Soviet Union in 1962. He joined the Soviet secret police, the KGB, in 1986. Five years later, the Soviet Union broke up. Litvinenko joined the Russian secret service, the FSK (FSB from 1995). In 1998, Litvinenko accused his superiors of ordering the assassination of a wealthy Russian businessman, Boris Berezovsky. Litvinenko was placed under arrest.

Alexander Litvinenko, his wife Marina, and son Tola photographed in Holland Park, London, in November 2000.

SEEKING ASYLUM

Litvinenko fled Russia with his wife and five-year-old son in 2000. After a brief stay in Turkey, they flew to London in November. Litvinenko applied to the British authorities for political asylum. He became a British citizen in 2006.

On November 1, 2006, Litvinenko suddenly fell ill. He was admitted to London's Barnet General Hospital. On November 17, the doctors transferred him to London's University College Hospital. At first, they thought he had been poisoned with thallium. Litvinenko had lost a huge amount of weight and was losing his hair. Toxicology tests were carried out.

Litvinenko died on November 23. Before his death, he told the authorities that he was sure he had been poisoned.

DELIBERATELY POISONED?

Health experts believed Litvinenko had been deliberately poisoned by a **radioactive** material called **polonium-210**. Traces of this substance were found in a sushi bar where he had dined and in the hotel where Litvinenko had attended some meetings on November 1. They also found traces at his home.

These are discs of polonium-210. Polonium-210 is an isotope of the element polonium and is a powerful emitter of alpha particle radiation.

WHAT IS POLONIUM-210?

Polonium-210 is an element that was discovered by Marie Curie in 1898. Small amounts of it are naturally present in the soil and in the air. Everyone has a small amount of it in their body, but not enough to damage tissues or organs. Additional polonium-210 would have to be digested or inhaled into the body to cause damage. It cannot pass through the skin.

A DEADLY TRAIL

Tests were carried out on all those who had come into contact with Litvinenko. The police confirmed that traces of polonium-210 had been found in three places in London. Traces were also found on two British planes at Heathrow Airport. By February 8, 2007, they had discovered 15 other people with more than the usual amounts of polonium-210 in their bodies—although not enough to harm them.

Detectives followed the forensic trail of polonium-210 around London and Europe. Polonium-210 gives out radioactive alpha particles. These can be stopped by human skin or even a piece of paper, but they can kill if swallowed. The polonium-210 that entered Litvinenko's body would have traveled in his blood. The alpha particles it emitted would have killed his cells and attacked and destroyed his organs.

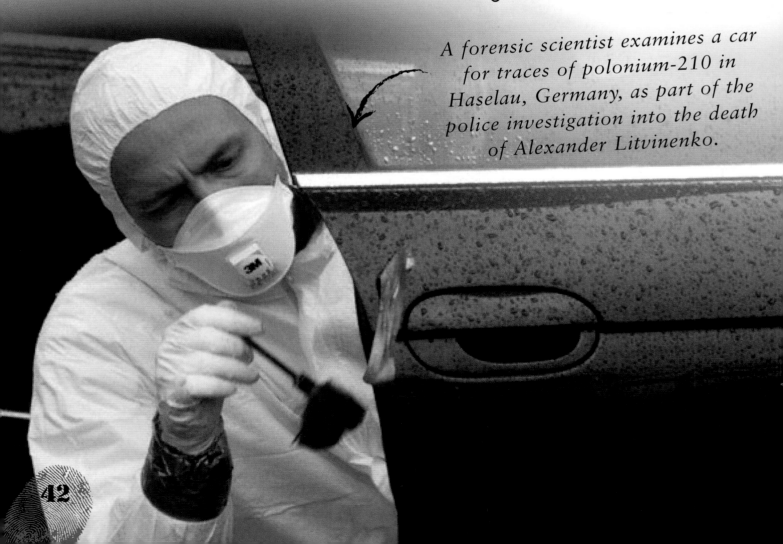

A forensic scientist examines a car for traces of polonium-210 in Haselau, Germany, as part of the police investigation into the death of Alexander Litvinenko.

Andrei Lugovoi, businessman and former KGB officer, is suspected by British police of poisoning Alexander Litvinenko.

A POT OF TEA

The police identified a man they believed to have poisoned Litvinenko. Andrei Lugovoi was a former KGB agent who had met with Litvinenko the day he fell ill. Logovoi was captured on cameras at Heathrow. He had arrived in London on a forged passport. The police believed Lugovoi slipped the poison into a pot of tea he made for Litvinenko in a London hotel room. He vanished hours after giving the polonium-210 to Litvinenko.

WHAT DO SCIENTISTS DO WITH BODY FLUIDS?

Body fluids include sweat, earwax, urine, blood, and saliva. These are useful to forensic scientists and pathologists. They can tell from body fluids how someone may have been poisoned or even who might have been the killer. The fluids are collected from the victim and suspect and put into airtight vials. The fluids are tested for the presence of poison. If traces of the poison are found in the suspect's sample, this provides evidence of the suspect's link to the crime.

TIME LINE

1750s   Dr. Hermann Boerhaave discovers that poisons can be identified by burning them and testing the gases that are produced.

1752   Mary Blandy stands trial for the murder of her father—the first poisoning trial involving forensic evidence. Four doctors carry out an autopsy of Mr. Blandy's body and find traces of arsenic powder.

1806   Valentine Rose shows how arsenic can be found in the human body.

1813   Mathieu Orfila experiments on animals to prove that after arsenic is taken into the body, it travels through all the organs.

1830s   James Marsh establishes the Marsh Test for identifying arsenic. Mathieu Orfila uses the Marsh Test to test the soil in cemeteries for arsenic. This helps when bodies need to be exhumed. If the body contains arsenic but the soil does not, the contamination must have occured before death.

1840   Marie LaFarge stands trial for the poisoning of her husband. Mathieu Orfila detects the presence of arsenic in the body of Charles LaFarge. He tests the soil in the cemetery. It is free from any trace of arsenic.

1900   Russian botanist Mikhail Tsvet invents the first chromatography technique.

1910   Dr. William Willcox, a British government toxicologist, helps prove that Dr. Hawley Crippen poisoned his wife.

1911 Dr. William Willcox carries out tests on the body of Elizabeth Barrow. He demonstrates how much arsenic the murderer Frederick Seddon used to poison her.

1935 The first scanning electron microscope image is created.

1950s The first gas chromatography technique is developed by Roland Gohlke and Fred McLafferty.

1957 Toxicologists in northern England find insulin in the body of Mrs. E. Barlow, who had been found dead in the bath. Her husband, a trained nurse, had poisoned her by injecting her with insulin.

1995 A Japanese cult releases the nerve gas sarin on the Tokyo underground, killing 12 and injuring thousands. Forensic toxicology tests identify the nerve gas.

1996 A high-speed gas chromatography mass spectrometer becomes available. This allows tests to be carried out in 90 seconds rather than 16 minutes.

1998 Forensic toxicologists prove that a number of Harold Shipman's victims had been injected with morphine.

2004 The president of Ukraine is poisoned with dioxin during his election campaign. Forensic tests show that he had more than a thousand times the usual amount in his body.

2004 In Japan, forensic evidence helps to convict a male nurse of murdering 10 people. He had given them muscle relaxants. These are poisonous if they are not needed for a medical condition because they restrict breathing.

2006 Toxicologists in Russia run tests on fake bottles of alcohol. They discover cleaning fluids, window deicer, and chemicals used for removing rust.

45

GLOSSARY

antimony
Antimony is silver-white and shiny in appearance. It is toxic. Antimony poisoning is very similar to arsenic poisoning. In small doses, antimony can cause headaches, dizziness, and depression. Larger doses cause violent vomiting, and death can occur.

arsenic
Arsenic is colorless and has no smell or taste. It can kill quickly if taken in large amounts. It is also deadly if given in small amounts over a long period.

autopsy
An examination of a dead body in order to establish the cause and circumstances of death.

belladonna
All parts of the belladonna plant are poisonous to humans. It is also known as deadly nightshade. Holding the leaf of the plant can cause blistering on the hands.

chromatography
A process that separates the components of a mixture.

Cold War
The long period of hostility (approximately 1945–90) between the United States, the Soviet Union, and their respective allies. It is described as "cold" because there was no actual fighting between the two main powers, but a tense battle for superiority.

cyanide
Cyanide has been used many times throughout history for poisoning. The most famous cyanides are hydrogen cyanide, potassium cyanide, and sodium cyanide. If swallowed, cyanide causes breathing problems, then affects the heart and leads to death.

digitalis
All parts of the digitalis plant are poisonous if eaten. It grows in many gardens and is also called foxglove.

enzymes
Enzymes are found in all living cells. They help control the metabolism and break down food.

ethylene glycol
Ethylene glycol is a colorless, odorless syrupy liquid with a sweet taste. It is used to make antifreeze.

exhume
The process of digging up a buried body to analyze why death occured.

forensics
Forensics is short for forensic science. Forensic science is the application of scientific techniques in the course of a criminal investigation. Types of forensic science include toxicology, serology (the study of body fluids), and ballistics (the study of guns and other firearms).

gas chromatography
A process that can analyze the components of a gas by injecting it into the stream of another inert (non-reactive) gas and into a long, thin tube that slows down each component. As the components emerge separately at the end of the tube, they pass through a detector that analyzes them.

hypodermic needle
A thin, hollow needle used with a syringe to give an injection.

insulin
Insulin is a hormone. It is given to diabetics to control the amount of sugar in their body's cells.

isotope
A version of an element that has the same number of protons but a different number of neutrons in the nucleus.

mass spectrometer
A piece of equipment that identifies the different ingredients within fluid mixtures. It is usually used with a gas chromatograph.

morphine
A painkilling drug obtained from opium. Morphine is prescribed by a doctor.

nuclear radiation
Particles emitted from the nucleus of unstable radioactive atoms.

pathologist
A scientist who conducts autopsies on bodies.

polonium-210
A rare radioactive metallic element. There are small amounts in the soil and atmosphere, but it is only dangerous if taken in high doses.

prescription
A written order issued by a doctor authorizing a pharmacist to provide a patient with a particular drug.

prosecution
Legal proceedings against someone who is suspected of breaking the law. It can also mean the lawyers representing the state or the people in a criminal trial.

psychiatrist
A doctor who treats mental illnesses.

radioactivity
The high-energy particles emitted by radioactive substances. A radioactive substance, such as polonium, emits a stream of high-energy particles due to the decaying of its unstable atoms.

ricin
Ricin comes from the castor oil plant. Tiny amounts of it can kill a person.

Soviet Union
Also called the USSR (Union of Soviet Socialist Republics), the Soviet Union was founded in 1922 as a communist state encompassing Russia and other nearby countries. It collapsed in 1991.

strychnine
A colorless, highly toxic drug that causes muscle spasms and death.

thallium
Thallium is a highly toxic substance that has no color, smell, or taste. It was once used in pesticides.

toxicology
The scientific study of poisons, especially their effects on the body and their antidotes.

white cell count
The number of white blood cells in a person's body.

FURTHER INFORMATION

BOOKS
Crime Scene: True-life Forensic Files #2: Profilers And Poison
by D.B. Beres and Anna Prokos, Scholastic, 2008

Drugs, Poisons and Chemistry (Essentials of Forensic Science)
by Suzanne Bell, Facts on File, 2008

Toxic!: Killer Cures and Other Poisonings
by Susie Hodge, Capstone Press, 2009.

WEB SITES
http://www.all-about-forensic-science.com/science-for-kids.html
This site provides information about forensic toxicology and forensic psychology.

http://www.cbc.ca/news/background/poison/
This site provides cases of famous people who were poisoned.

www.buzzle.com/articles/forensic-toxicology.html
This site gives you links to information on forensic science and forensic toxicology.

www.forcon.ca/learning/forensic_toxicology.html
This is a forensic toxicology consultancy. The Web site has information on different types of toxicology. It also explains how tests are carried out.

47

INDEX